Presented to:

Marcia and Rob

By

Mom and Dad Cannon

Given to you as you grow together from February 17 '91 on... may your deep contentment and love for each other always be like a February spring. Each page of this book speaks truth and experience and I pray the pages will be meaningful to you both.

We love you,

BEGINNINGS
FOR THE NEWLY MARRIED

Judith Mattison

Augsburg Publishing House
Minneapolis, Minnesota

Beginnings

Copyright © 1980 Augsburg Publishing House

Library of Congress Catalog Card No. 79-54114

International Standard Book No. 0-8066-1753-5

All rights reserved. No part of this book may be used or reproduced in any manner whatsoever without written permission except in the case of brief quotations embodied in critical articles and reviews.
For information address Augsburg Publishing House, 426 South Fifth Street, Minneapolis, Minnesota 55415.

Photos and design by Koechel/Peterson Design, Minneapolis, Minnesota.

Manufactured in the United States of America.

To Anne and Mark Wiberg,
who show me what marriage can be—
sharing, laughing, supporting,
forgiving, accepting, telling the truth,
trying again, bound in God's grace,
and filled with love.

Beginnings

Marriage isn't just a ceremony. Marriage is a covenant,
a decision to learn to live together and to perfect the love we share.

We can't know what lies ahead. We know only that we will share it,
and that God will be there to support us and love us
through both good and bad times.

We understand each other more fully as we begin to share
our daily routines, our deepest thoughts and our varied emotions,
our weak moments and our strengths. We help and encourage and learn
from each other. Little by little, we grow.

Marriage is more than a ceremony.
It is a beginning.
We are beginning a new life — together.

*The beauty of a wedding
Is love,
Evident;
Shining—
Promises given and renewed,
The joy of God's presence
Among us.*

*Opening wedding gifts
Is like February spring!
People have been kind, generous,
Sharing our joy.
We send our thanks
    to them
    and God,
Aware that our greatest gift
Is our love.*

I watch you
      brushing your teeth
      sitting quietly
      eating
      sleeping.
I am pleased
To see you
And to know how close
We have become
And how much closer
We may yet grow.

*I knew I loved you
When we talked for hours
As we walked or drove
Or sat in a corner
And forgot others were there.
It has not changed.
Our best times
Are long talks.*

*Other people smile
When we act silly.
Perhaps they've forgotten
How much fun it is
To laugh at each other
And enjoy being together,
Childlike.
I pray we'll always cherish
This magic.*

Our household is
Second-hand furniture,
Unmatched china,
Leftover comfort,
And appointed in
Hand-me-downs.
I seldom notice
Because it's ours.

What would I do if you died?
A gasp of fear
Empties my chest
And I reach to know
You are there.
I am more dependent
Than I've ever been before.
Growing together, we risk
The deepest sorrow
We will ever know.

We could ignore little irritating habits
When we parted each day.
Now differences in personal routines
Gnaw at our patience and tolerance.
We search for ways to say
    I'm annoyed.
    That bothers me.
Challenging each other's habits,
We both find ways to change.
Other things we learn to accept—
Not in resignation,
But in understanding.

I do not know you.
There is a space inside you,
A sheltered grotto
You must keep private.
It is the mystery of you
Which will continue to intrigue me
As you unfold before me.

I'm surprised to discover
That I need time
Away from you.
It worried me at first:
I wondered if it was
A sign of waning love.
But my trip was fun.
I learned a lot:
I like myself better—
And I love coming home
To you!

*It seems to me,
I've never cried so often
Or so hard.
I have a driving need
To find a way for us
To live together
Without destroying me,
Or you.
But when it's hard,
I cry.
I think it's a sign
That I care.*

*Rainstorm
Drenches us.
Laughing,
We run to shelter.
Your face is shiny wet
And your hands cool.
Our embrace
Is like forgiveness.
I am refreshed
And warm.*

*It's hard to realize
There is as much need
For no
And why
As there is for yes
And happy.
Marriage is not a magic elixir
For joy and satisfaction.
It is a watercolor painting.
The light and dark colors
    of experience
Blend and accent one another
As we share
All that life offers us.*

*It used to be significant
To go with a date to church—
A special occasion,
A mark of respectful attention.
Now that I belong beside you,
When we're in church
We are more uniquely individual
Yet more united
Than at any other time.*

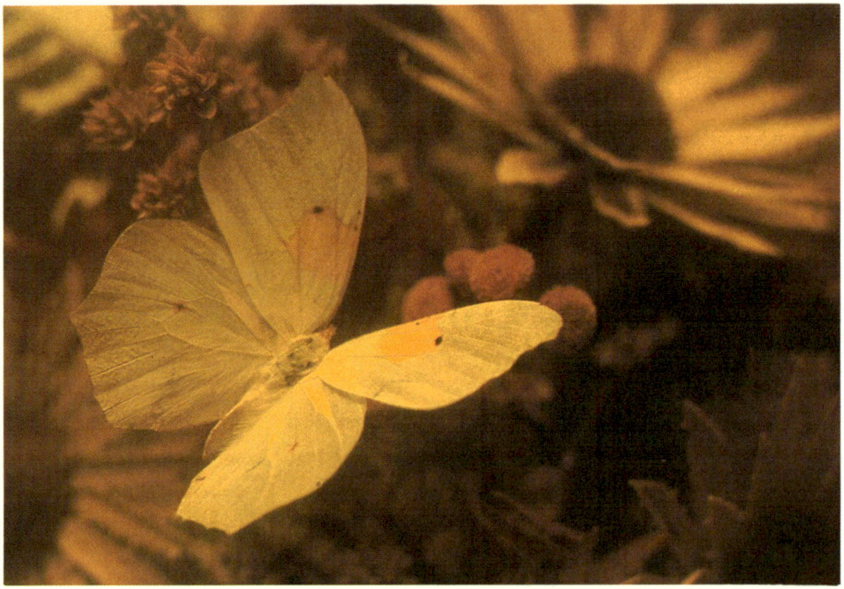

*My love for you
Is sometimes so great,
So filling,
That I feel able to fly!
Has anyone known this love before?
Perhaps, but it doesn't matter.
This feeling is ours,
Stronger than hunger
And deeper than words can say.
God gives us a glimpse of joy,
Larger than life
And stronger than all winds of change
I love you, I love you, I love you!*

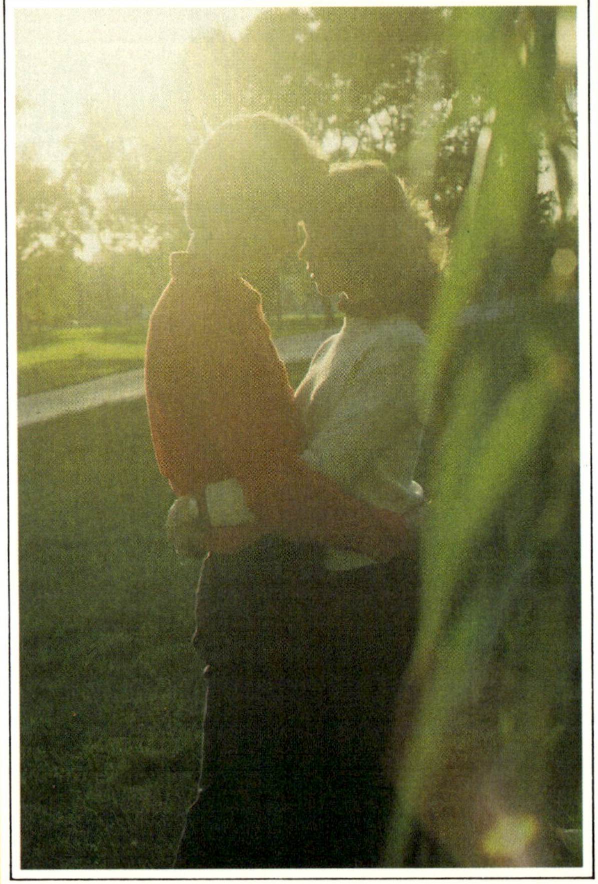

Come and let me hold you
In this time of disappointment.
Come and let me say
With words and touch
That I love you
When you feel you've failed.
Come and we will share this time,
However sad or painful.
It will help to have each other.
Come to me.

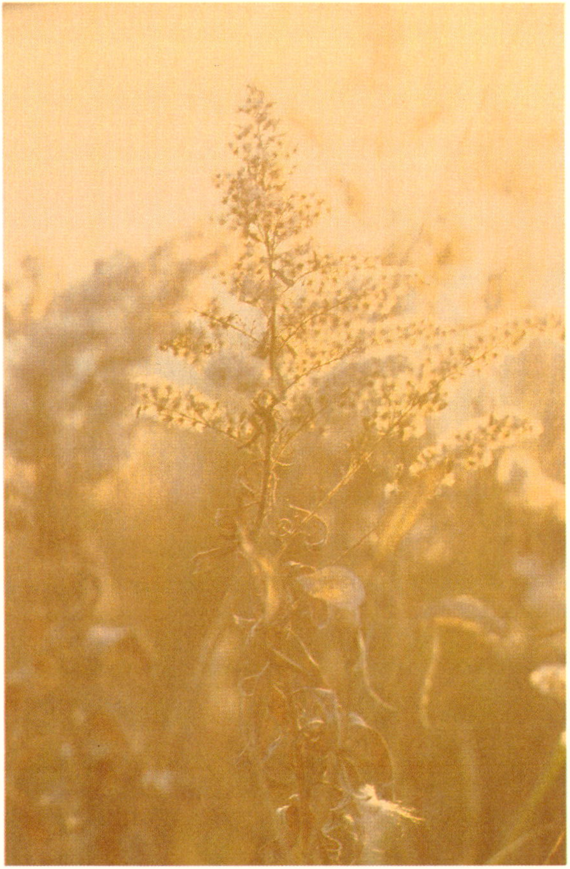

Your family,
My family,
Do not live here with us,
But I sense their presence
In small ways—
> *family habits you've acquired*
> *traditions I don't question*
> *roles and expectations.*

Often we must look carefully
To be sure we are we
> *not they.*

We must build our relationship
According to our needs
> *not theirs.*

We take the best of our separate pasts
And intertwine them
In our blessed todays.

*Frost paintings on the window.
Every day with you
A new design.
Discovery.*

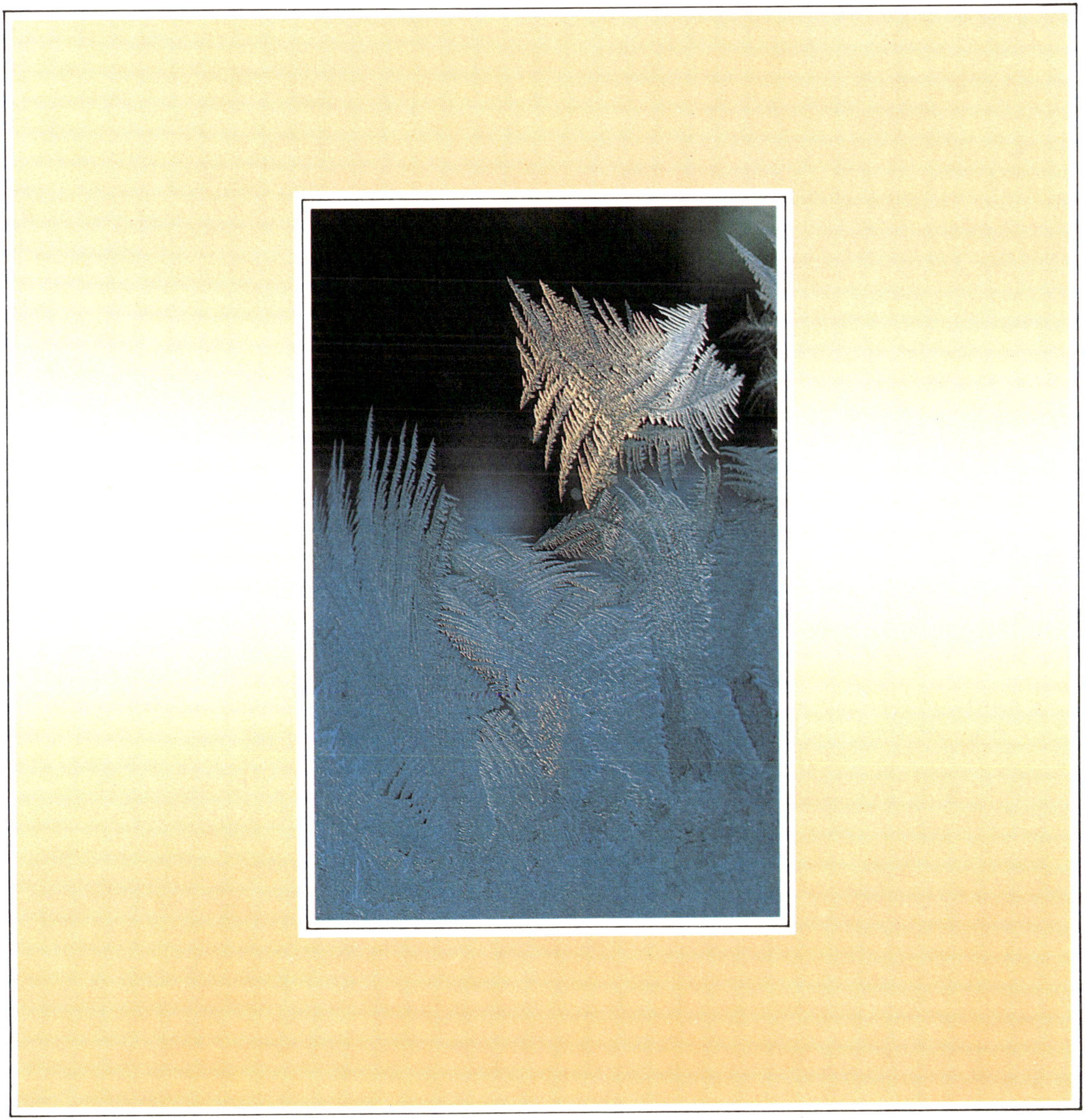

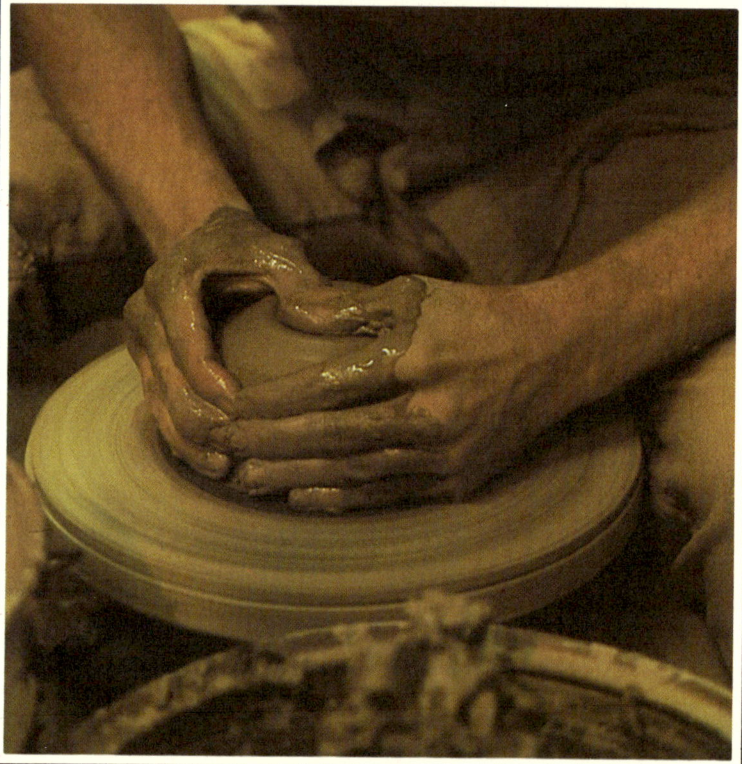

*I don't expect perfection
From most people
But sometimes I realize
I expect more of you
Than of anyone else.
I want to be proud of you
Because you're mine.
That's not fair.
I will try to change—
To love not only strength
But also my opportunity
To care in spite of weakness.*

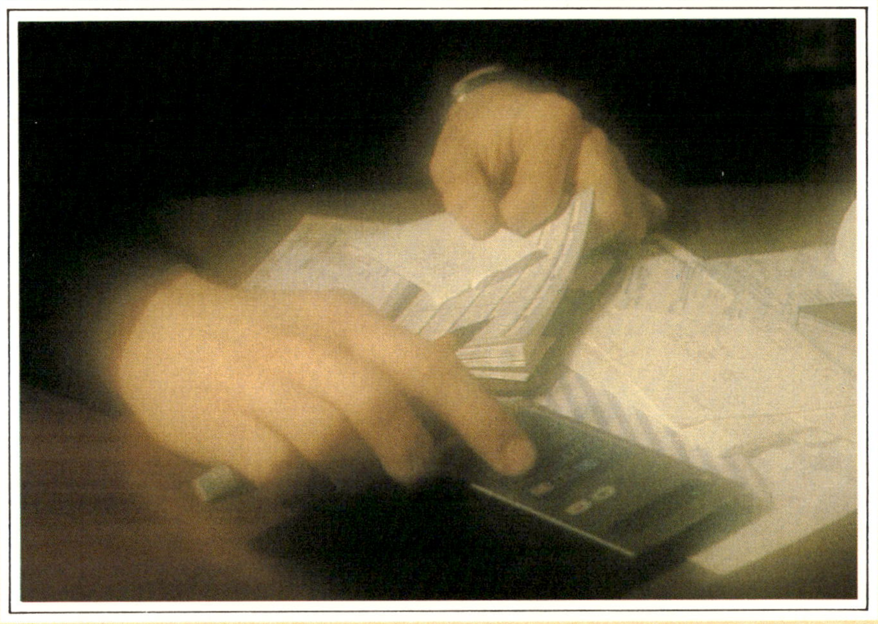

*I am sad
That we should argue
Over money.
Did I expect
That we would think alike
In every situation?
We do not live independent
Of the outside world.
But we will work it through—
As long as money
Is less important than
Caring conversation.*

Good morning!
I'm still surprised
To find you here
    beside me
    smiling.
My daylight awakening
Is always warm and sunny
When I discover you again.
We begin once more.

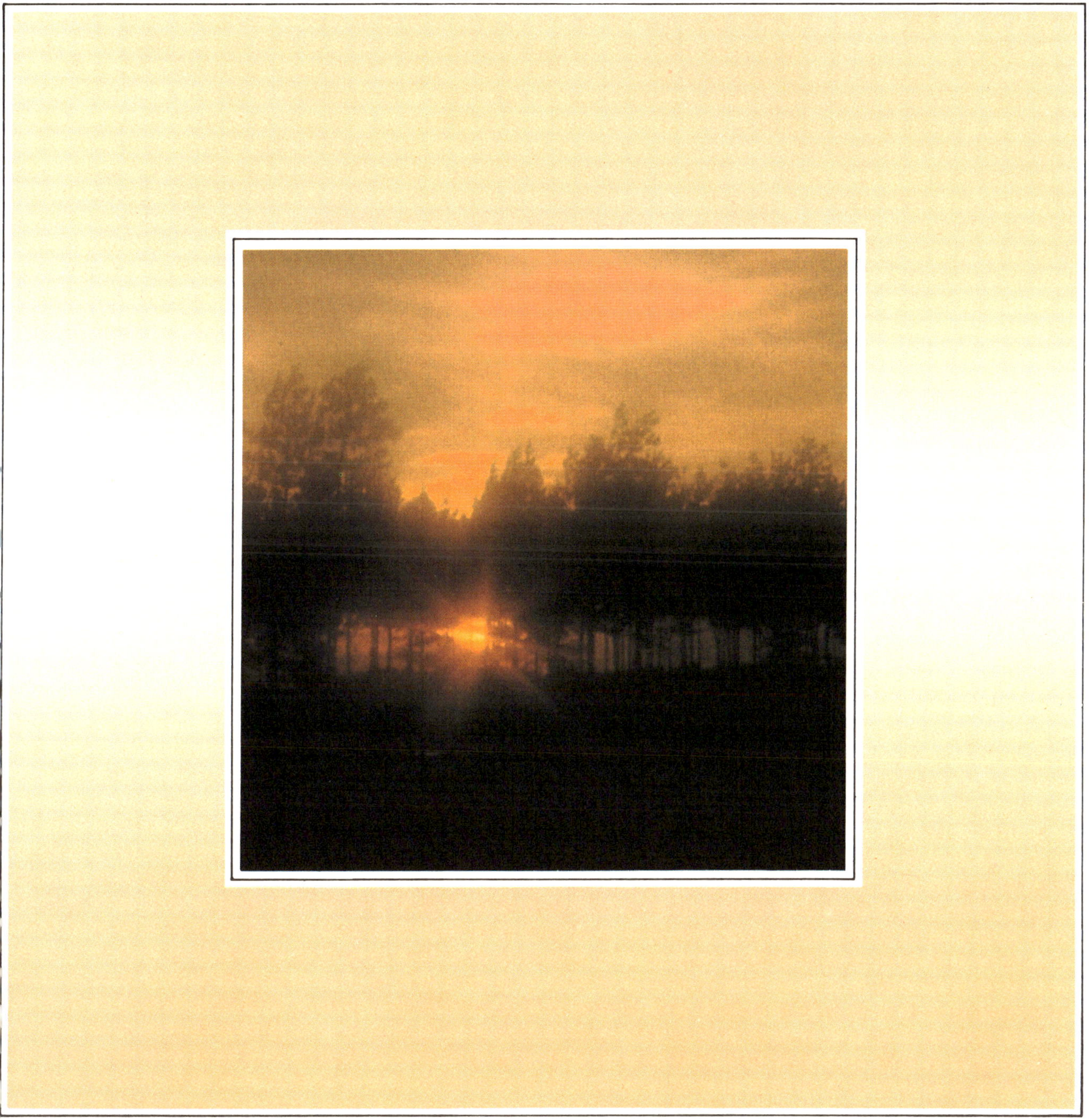

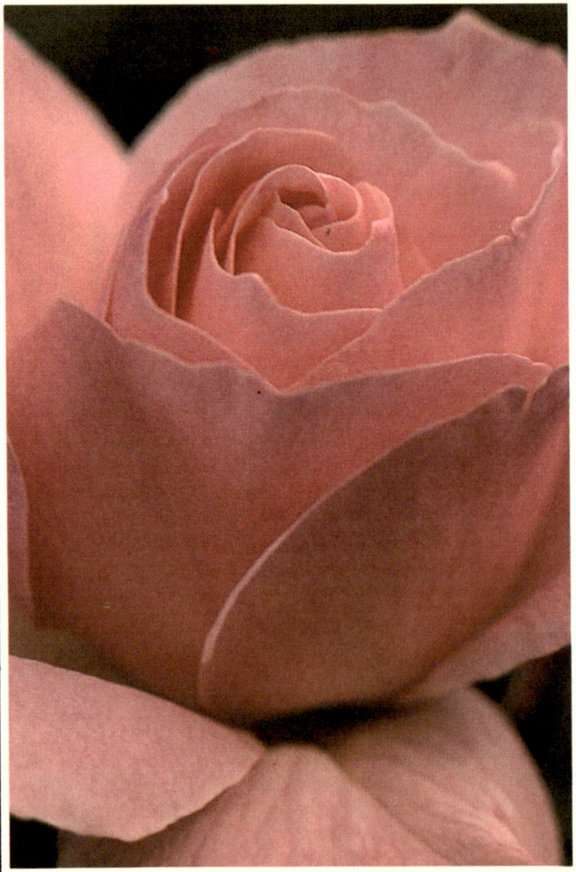

*You are not well.
My day is at odds with itself,
My mind distracted,
Picturing you at home alone,
Tired, restless, aching:
I want to be there with you,
To comfort and soothe.
I want always to be there when you need me.*

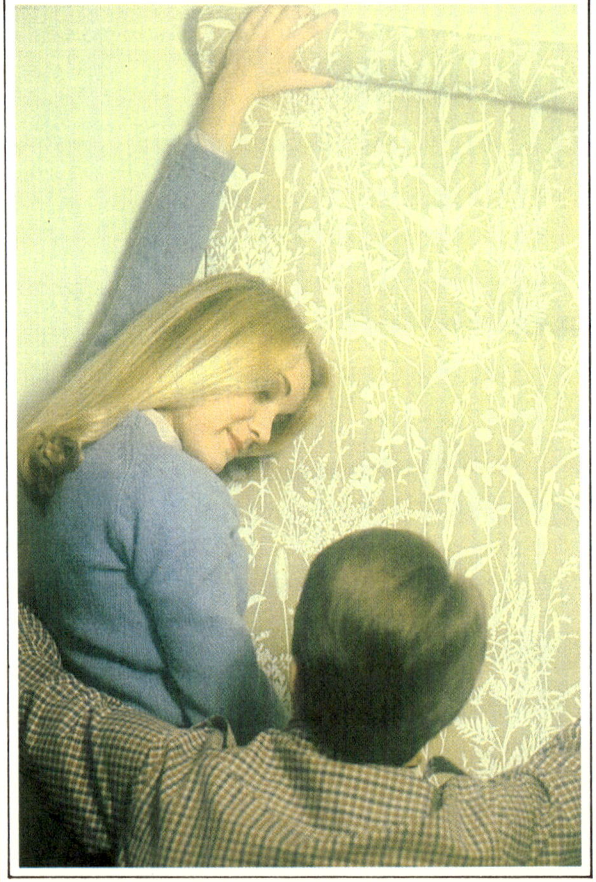

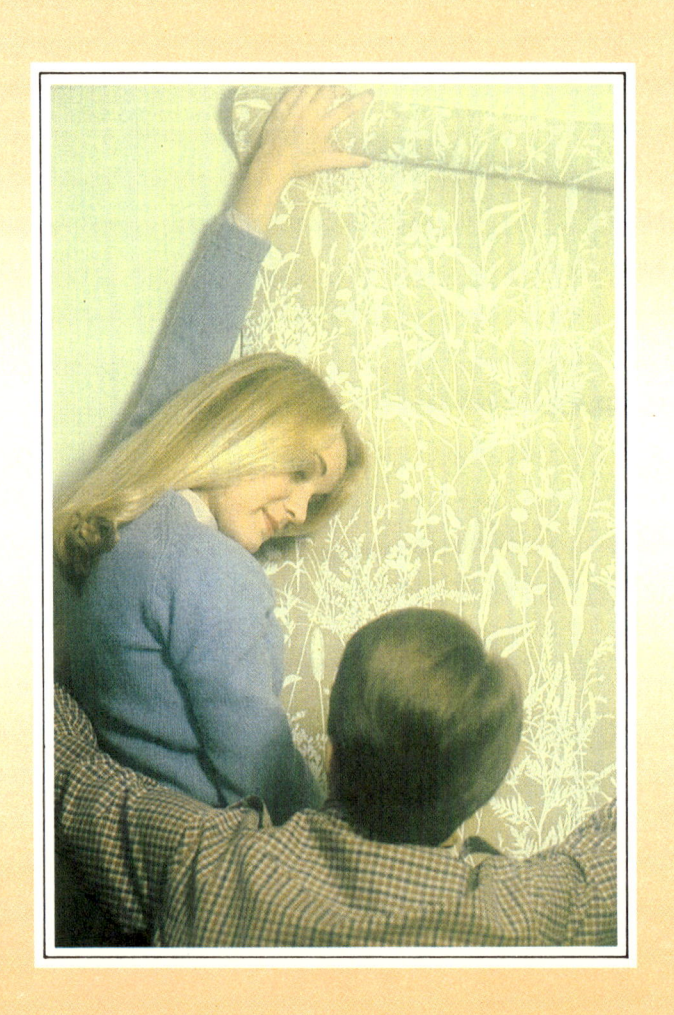

*When I have a job to do,
You come too—
    to hold the ladder
    or help clean up.
I no longer need to be
Earnest and efficient.
With you here helping, we
    laugh at mistakes
    cajole bad tempers
    finish in half the time.
Tasks are easier somehow,
With you.*

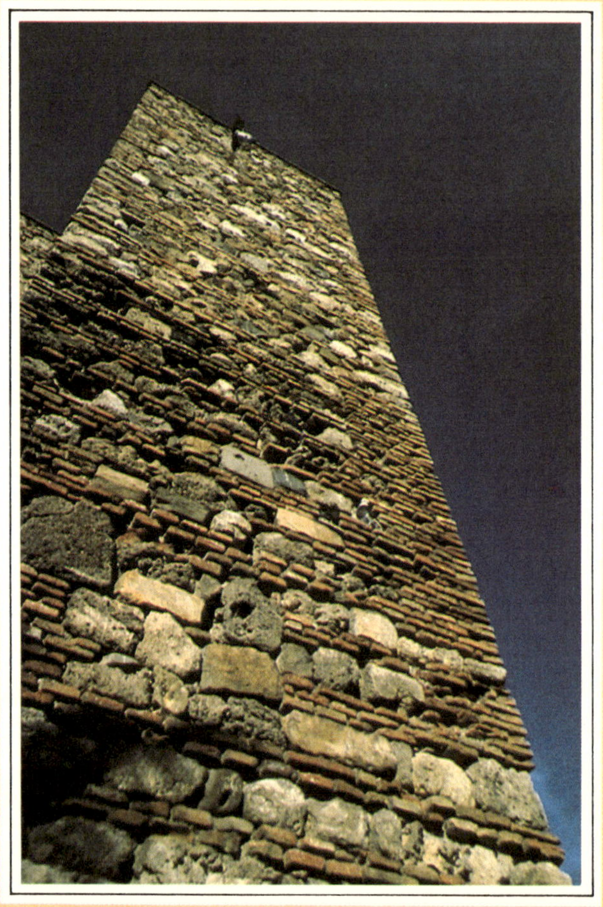

*We are not alike.
More and more we discover
Differences.
Your strength is often my lack,
And my spirit rises
When yours may be inclined to sag.
Together we build,
Mortar filling crevice,
Strength on strength,
Complementing one another
And appreciating the design
Where differences are as rich
As similarities.*

Guests complete our home.
We welcome them
And this chance to share
    our happiness
    our searching
    the new life we are forming.
Their laughter lingers
As we do dishes together,
Recalling the evening's warmth.
Guests have brightened our lives,
Leaving us happy
To be alone together again.

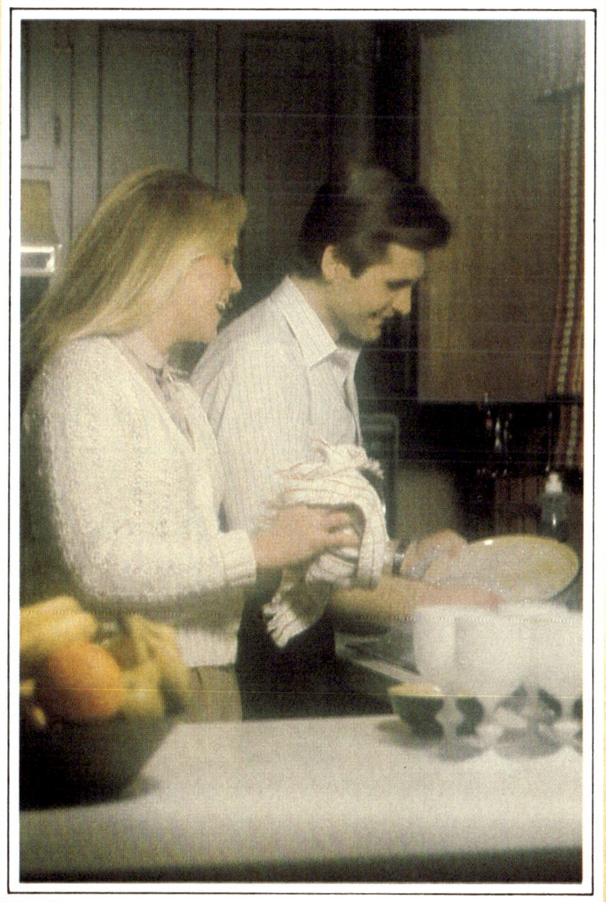

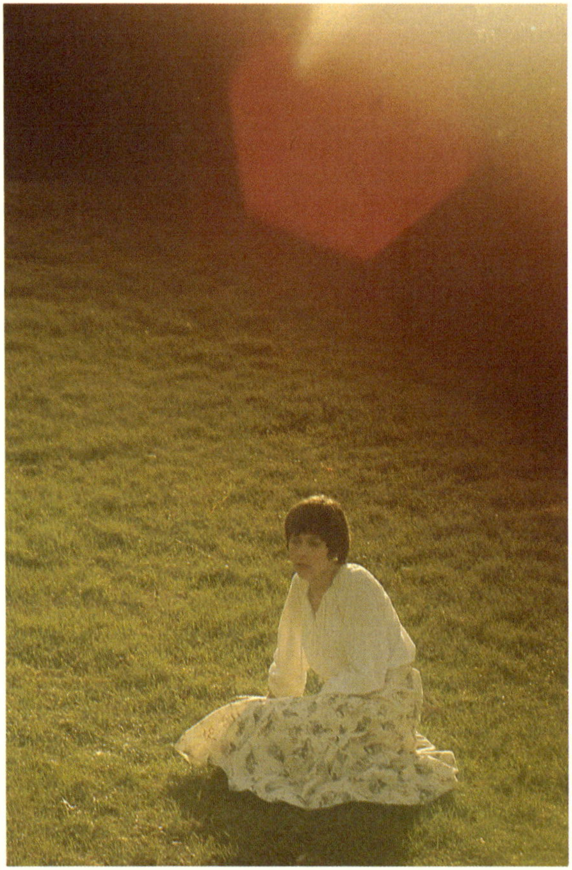

I'm dissatisfied.
It's hard to say it.
I'd rather overlook it.
But I've discovered problems don't go away.
Someday I must face my concern
And tell you how I feel.
I have to learn to trust that
You will hear my sincere caring
As well as my criticism or disappointment.
Love does not mean constant agreement.
Love means trusting and telling the truth.
I will tell you how I feel
Because I love you,
Because I trust that you will
Want to hear my honest self,
That you will try to understand.

*We walked downtown
Through the snow.
We laughed and talked,
Had ice-cream sundaes.
Our neighbor wondered
If we were tired and cold.
We had walked several miles!
But the time went fast
And we weren't tired at all.
We don't notice time or miles
When we're talking together.*

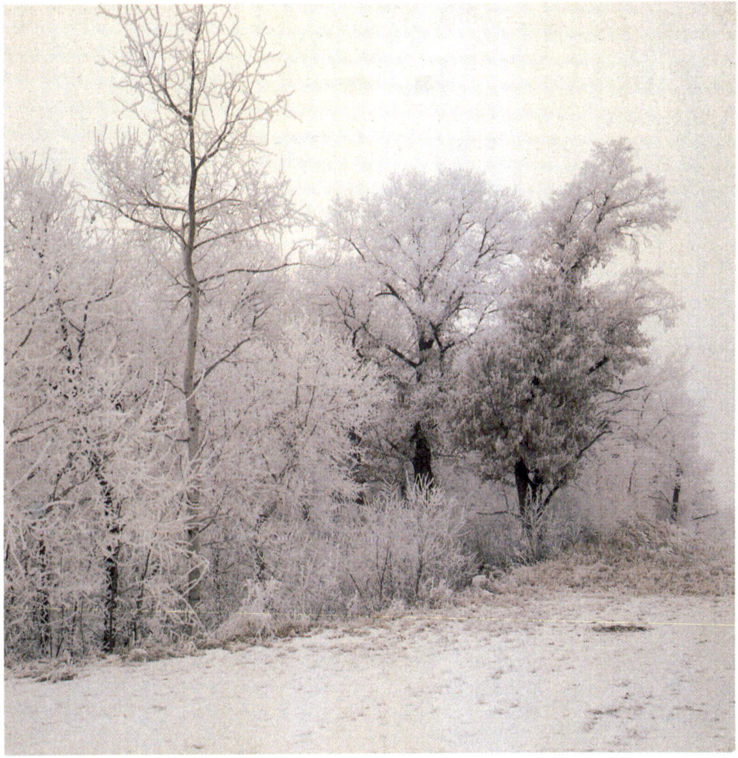

Fury!
Barbed-wire mentality.
I hated the sound of my voice
Screaming at you with my selfishness
And quavering in disappointment
As you retaliated.
Why did we allow our feelings
To overrule our promise
To try to hear and understand?
The pain as we retrace our fence
And mend the damage
Is poignant reminder
Of our foolish haste and need to win.
I'm sorry.

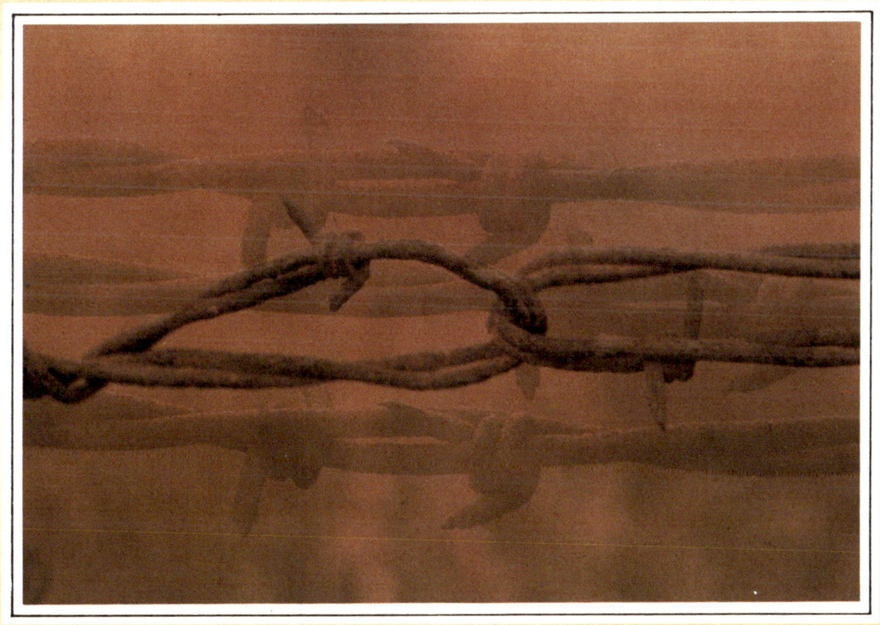

*You're good for me.
You help me laugh at*
    *my mistakes
    idiosyncrasies
    habits I've long since stopped examining.
I'm grateful there is someone who*
    *accepts my imperfections
    forgives
    ignores
Or gently helps me change.
I don't mind being less than perfect
When you are here beside me.*

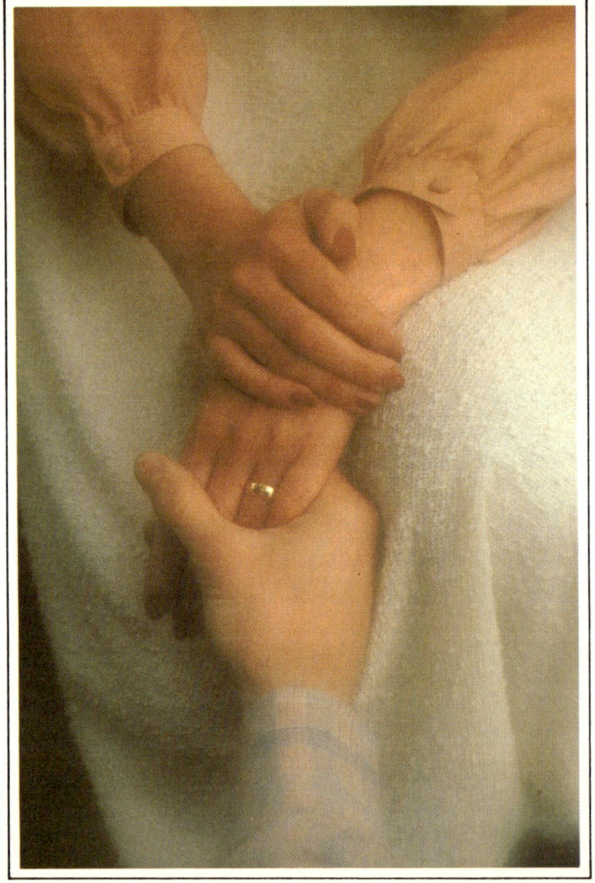

*Praying together
Adds new strength
To our lives.
I sense that God surrounds us,
Weaving his Spirit
Into our thoughts and words.
There is mystery
As two people
Share earnest caring
And searching,
Knowing God is greater—
    waiting
    listening
    and loving.*

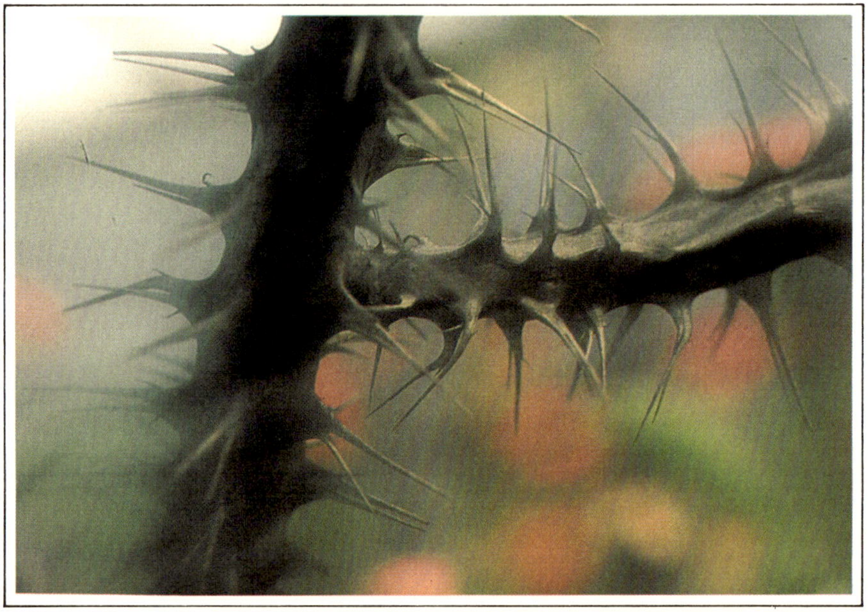

*You did not hear
What I tried to say.
I am misunderstood,
Hurt:
Help me not to blame
But to speak again
More clearly
In love.*

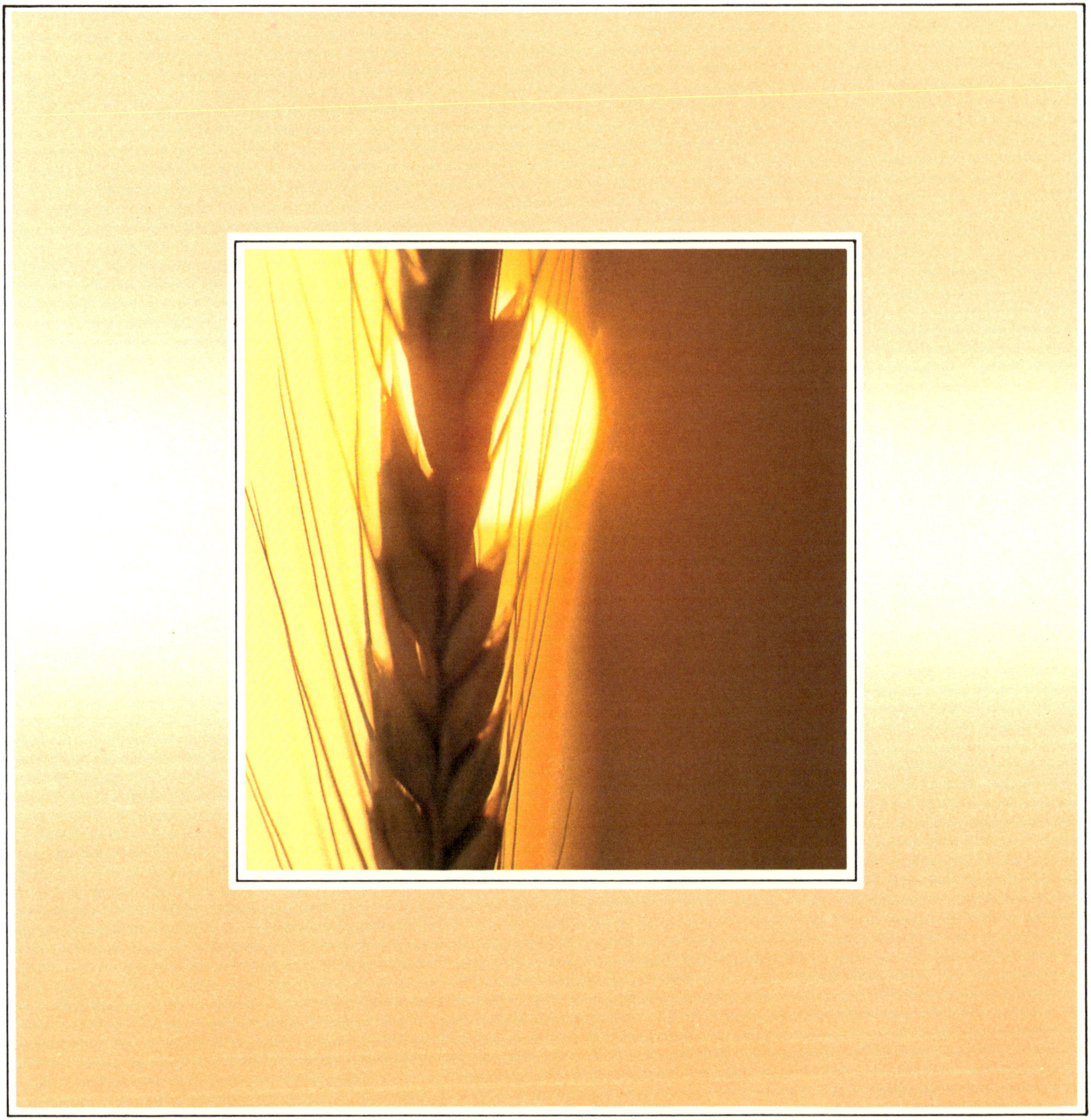

*It's hard to imagine,
Many years from now,
Who we'll be
Or where,
What we will have done
And known.
But I am eager
To be part of our future.
When years of shared experiences
Bind us together,
I pray we will not lose
The joy of discovering
Who we are,
How we change,
And all the reasons
We love each other.*

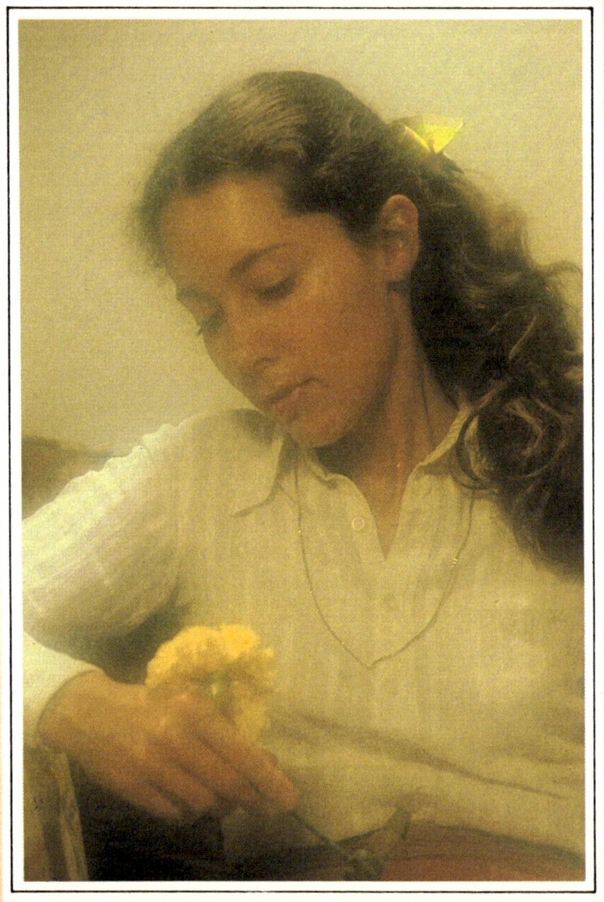

*Jealousy
Is the fear of losing
And the need to possess.
Tell me,
Show me,
Help me believe
You love me
And I need not cling
Or fear.*

*Life is filled with
    routine
    repetition
    familiarity.
Spring's budding trees
Bring the wonder of change.
We rejoice in newness.
You are my spring,
My hope for refreshment.
This is God's blessing on us—
That together we hope for
A better world,
A world of fresh beginnings.*

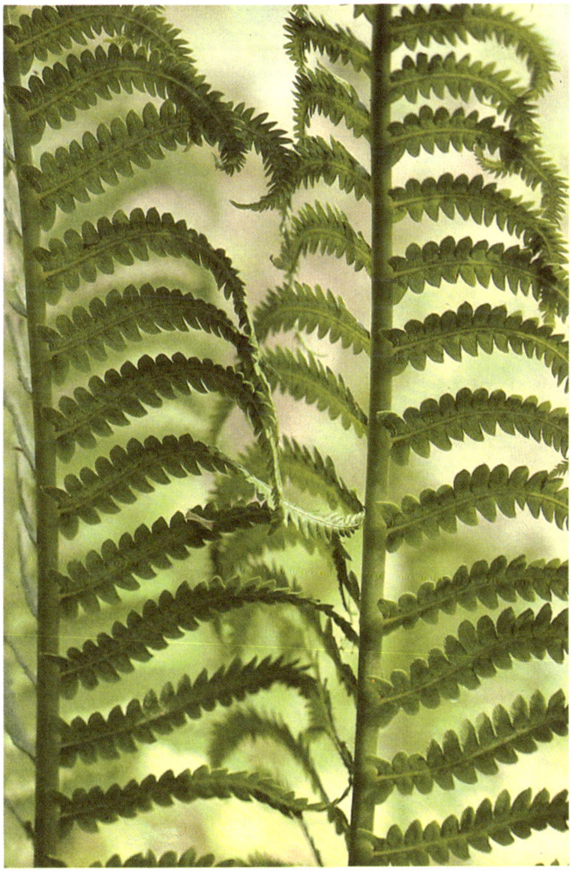

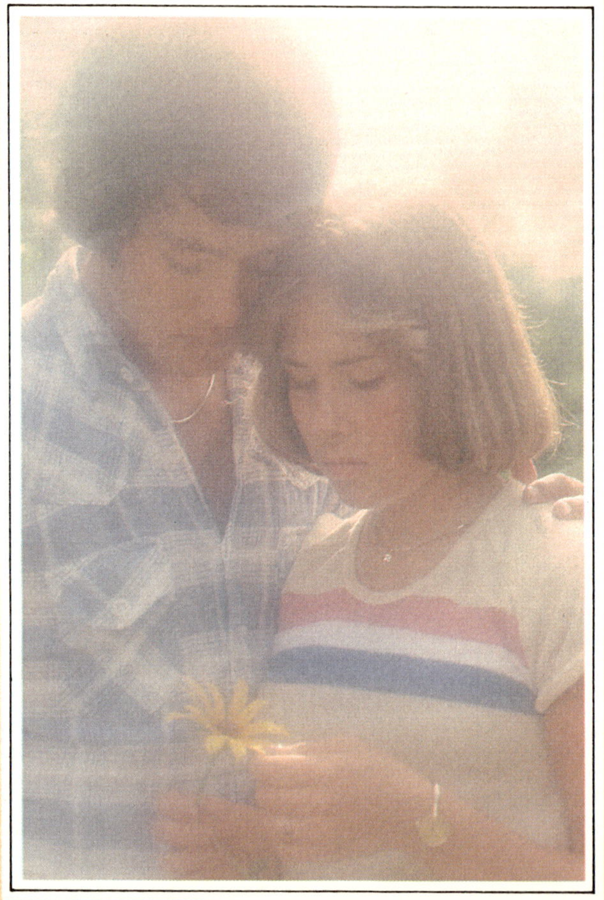

These have been labored hours,
Tense,
Quiet,
A fear-filled mystery.
Something happened
To unsettle our balance,
But no one spoke.
Now that we have talked it through,
Not only once, but several times,
We can go on.
We have learned that differences
Are not bridged
By silence.

When I feel proud of you
I nearly burst.
I'm delighted at your satisfaction,
Eager to wish you well.
Even though I know the achievement
Is yours alone,
I smile in your radiance
As if it were mine,
Sharing your accomplishments
With pride.

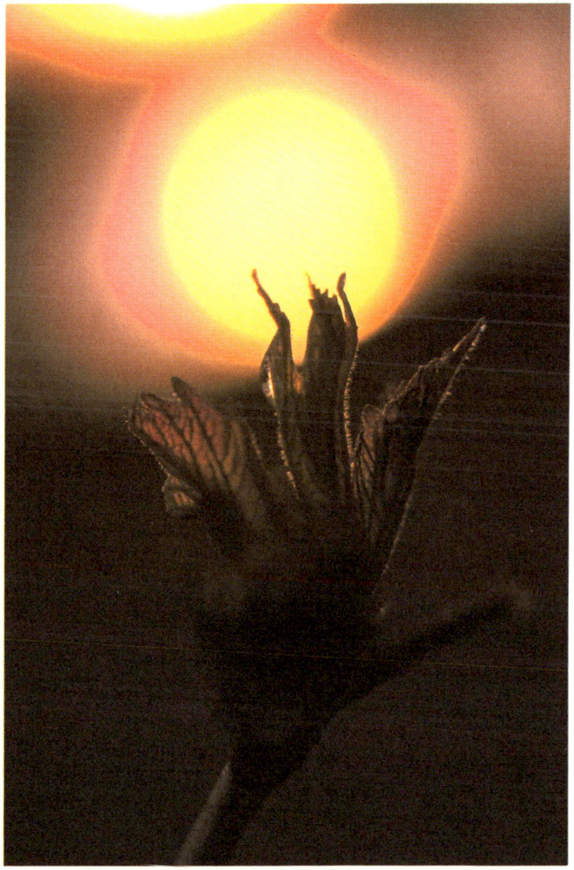

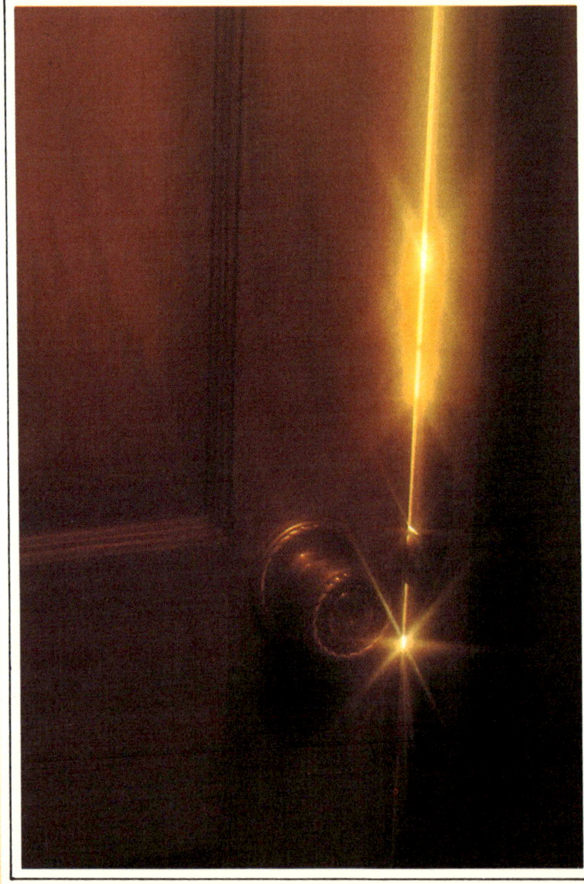

We've been distracted by
    noise
    people
    busy schedules.
We haven't had enough time
To talk and be together.
Let's not let distractions
Pull us apart.
Promise me we will always take time
To be alone together.
Let's run away—
Even if it's only behind
Our own locked door.

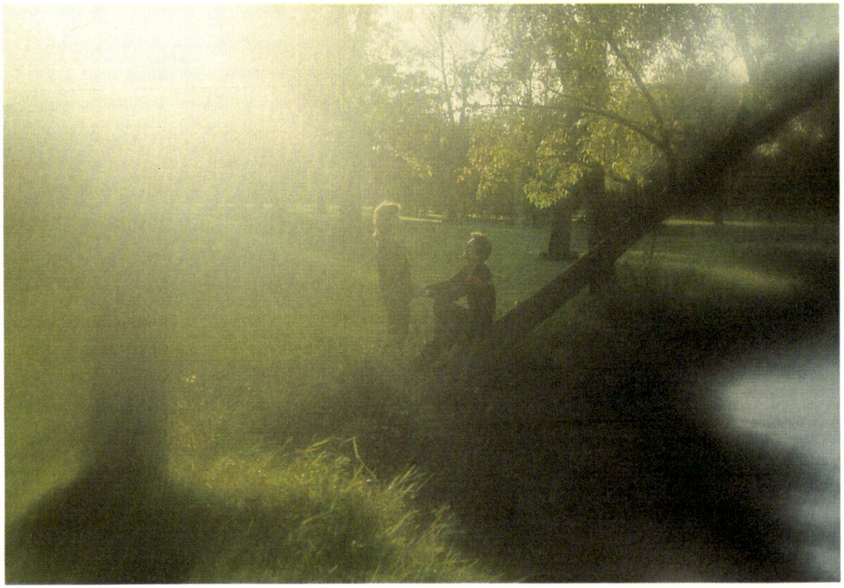

*I didn't realize
How good it would be
To help you lift your dulled spirits
With kindness or joking.
I always knew
You would comfort and encourage me.
I'm learning
That I'm glad to do the same
For you.*

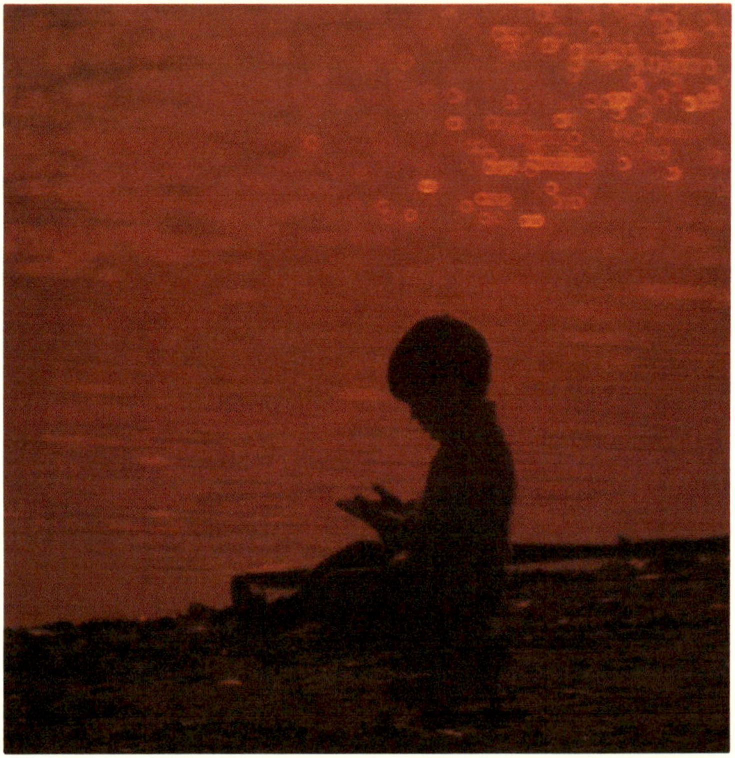

*Someday we may want
To be parents.
It's frightening—
Responsibility.
But watching you
    smiling
    talking
    playing with children
I think it may
Strengthen our bond
To have a child,
To join in that loving task.*

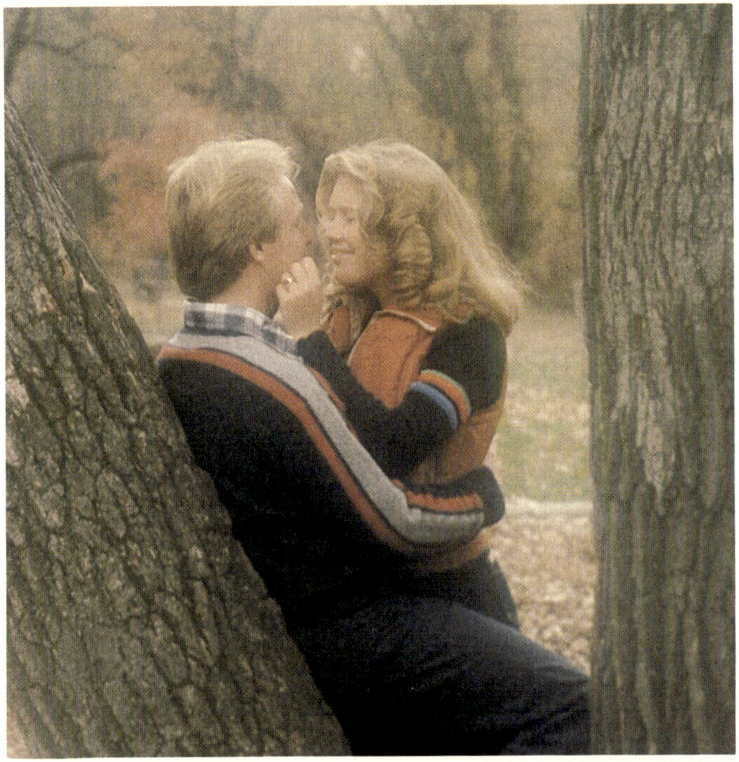

*Just when I think
I know you,
You surprise me with
    a new idea
    a silly thought
    a quiet word
To remind me
That the joy of living
Is the mystery of always
Discovering each other anew.*

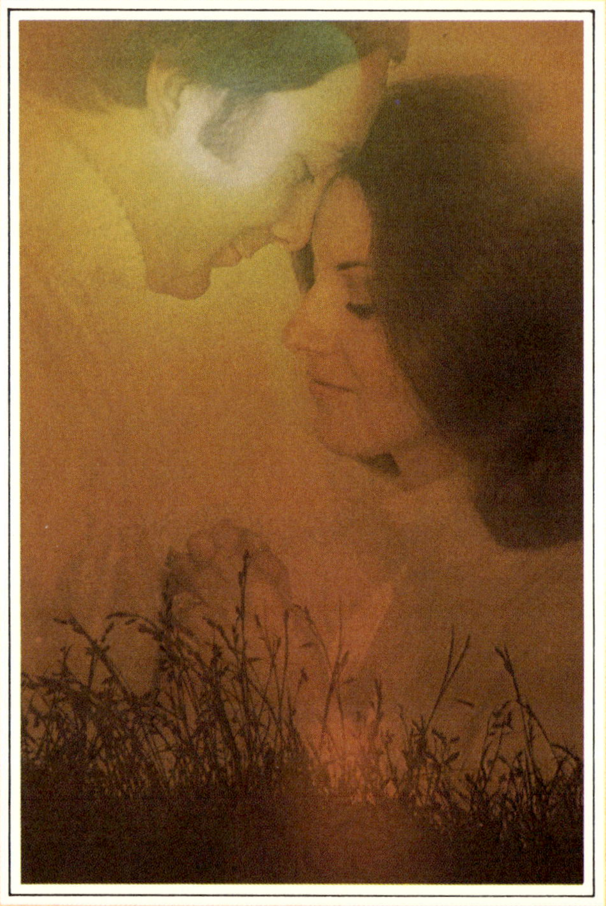

*I hinted for days.
I suppose I thought you would
    read my mind
    sense my need
    catch the clues.
You didn't;
And disappointment
Shaded my desire and words.
I finally told you what I need
    clearly
    directly
    without predetermining your answer.
Now you know.
Now we grow.*

*Maps ready and bags packed,
We are going on a trip—
Our very own!
We have planned and dreamed
And wondered what we'd see.
Starting off together
Is a genuine adventure.
We will see more than ever before
Because we will see with
Each other's eyes
As well as our own.
Glad, happy time in life!
We will look at God's world
With heightened expectation,
And the pleasure of doing it all
Together.*

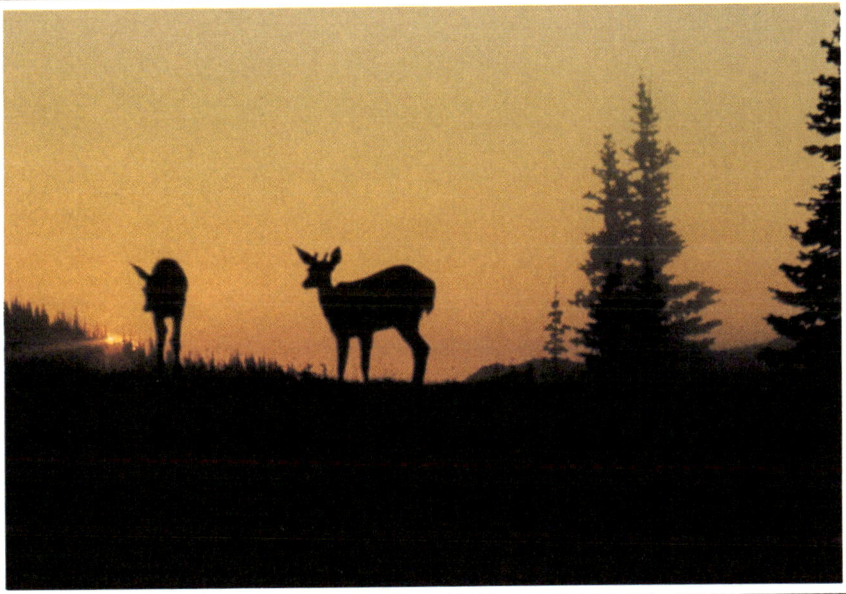

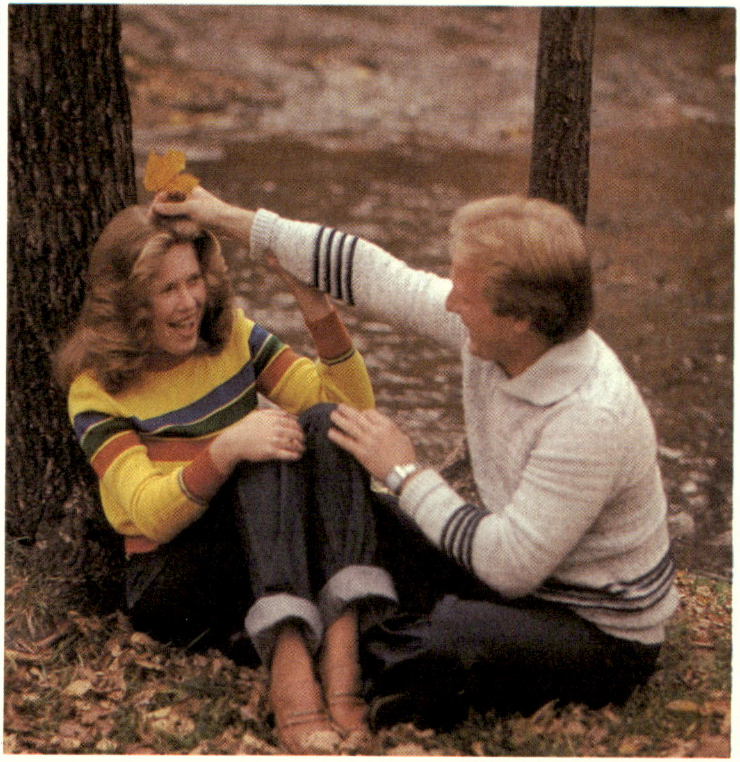

No one else makes me laugh as you do!
No one else shares so many of my secrets,
   my private jokes.
No one else knows my silly side,
Those little teasing thoughts
That bring a smile from my heart.
When we laugh
I feel I'm a child again,
   happy
   fresh
   and loved.

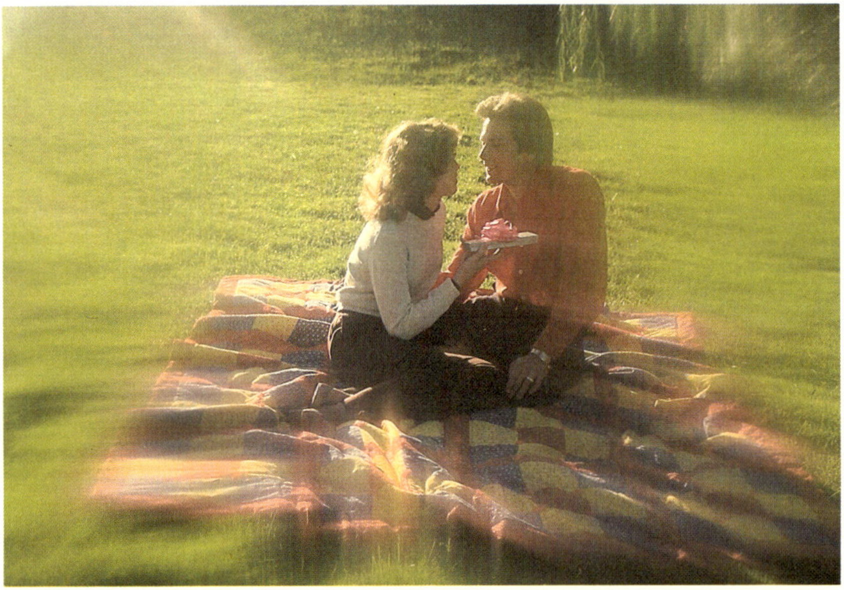

An anniversary gift
Will signify
That we have traveled
A whole year
Together.
I shall choose it carefully.
But the gift does not portray
The meaning of the journey.
The anniversary marks our growing,
The gift, my love,
Is you.